Numbers

Susan Canizares • Daniel Moreton

Scholastic Inc.

New York • Toronto • London • Auckland • Sydney

D0814316

Acknowledgments

Literacy Specialist: Linda Cornwell

Early Childhood Consultant: Ellen Booth Church

Design: Silver Editions

Photo Research: Silver Editions

Endnotes: Susan Russell

Endnote Illustrations: Ruth Flanigan

Photographs: Cover: Kunio Owaki/The Stock Market; p. 1: Kunio Owaki/The Stock Market; p. 2: Michael Newman/Photo Edit; pp. 3, 4, 5: David Young-Wolff/Photo Edit; p. 6: Jon Feingersh/The Stock Market; pp. 7, 10: Robert Brenner/Photo Edit; p. 8: Chuck Savage/The Stock Market; pp. 9, 12: Tony Freeman/Photo Edit; p. 11: Claire Hayden/Tony Stone Images.

No part of this publication may be reproduced in whole or in part, or stored in a retrieval system, or transmitted in any form or by any means, electronic, mechanical, photocopying, recording, or otherwise, without written permission of the publisher. For information regarding permission, write to Scholastic Inc., 555 Broadway, New York, NY 10012.

Library of Congress Cataloging-in-Publication Data
Canizares, Susan, 1960-
Numbers/Susan Canizares, Daniel Moreton.
p.cm. -- (Learning centers emergent readers)
Summary: Simple text and photographs explore some of the ways
we use numbers, from weights and measures to prices to telling time.
ISBN 0-439-04599-1 (pbk.: alk. paper)
1. Number concept--Juvenile literature.
[1. Number concept.] I. Moreton, Daniel. II. Title. III. Series.
QA141.3.C35 1999
513--dc21   98-54206
CIP AC

Copyright © 1999 by Scholastic Inc.
Illustrations copyright © 1999 by Scholastic Inc.
All rights reserved. Published by Scholastic Inc.
Printed in the U.S.A.

13 14 15 16 17 18 19 20   08   09 08 07 06

How do numbers help us?

Numbers help us buy things.

Numbers help us weigh things.

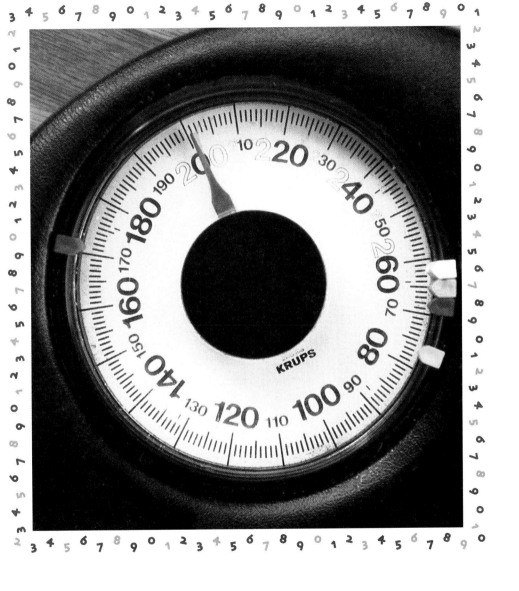

Numbers help us play games.

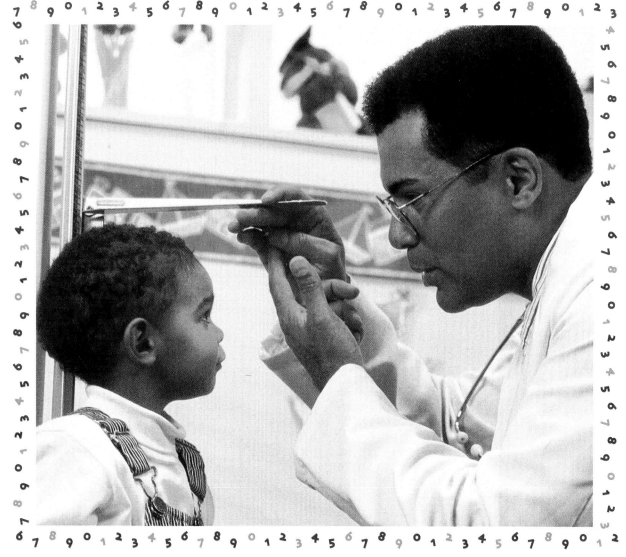

Numbers help us measure things.

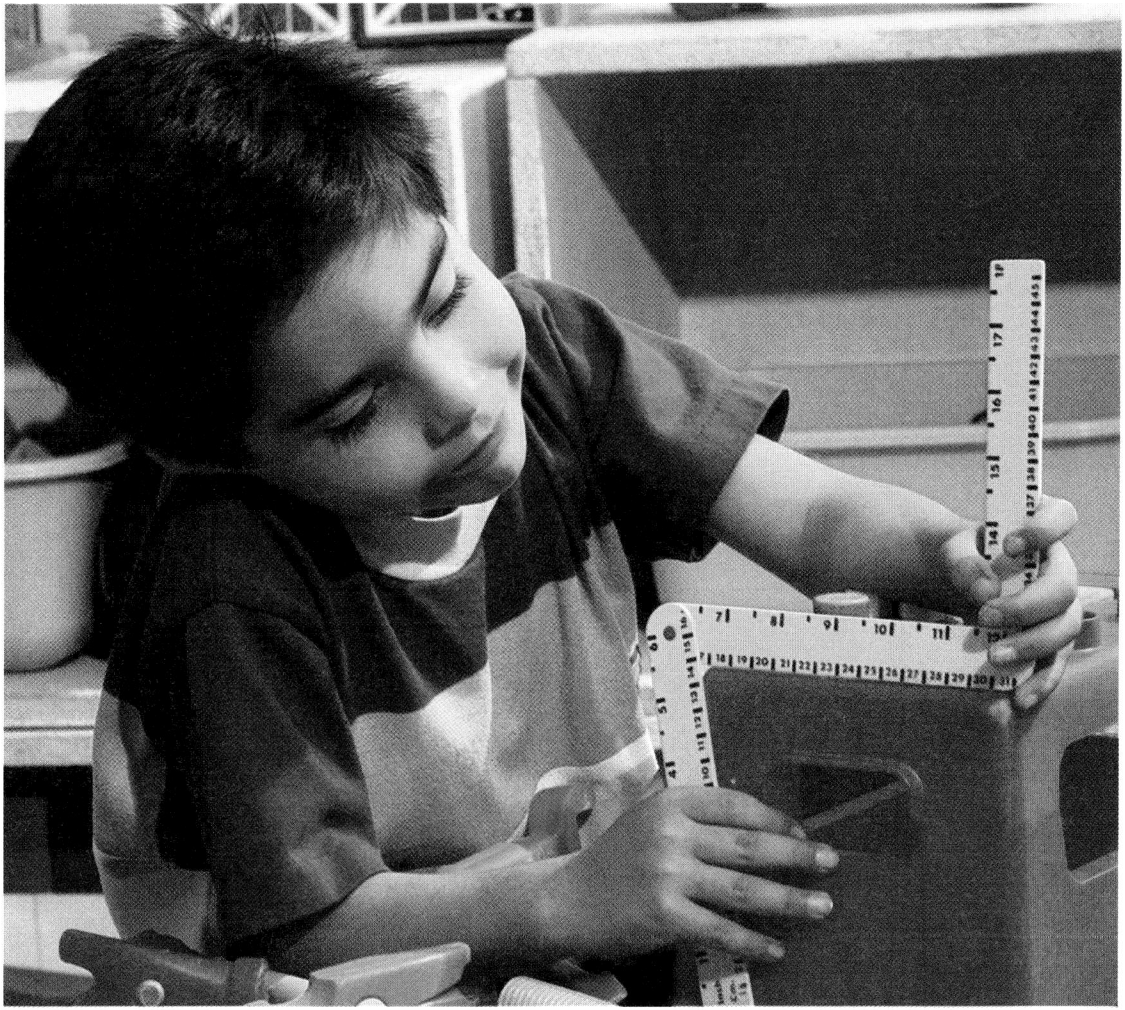

Numbers help us go places.

TAXI FARE

$2<u>00</u> Initial Charge

30¢ Per 1/5 Mile

20¢ Per Minute Stopped
or Slow Traffic

50¢ Night Surcharge

Numbers help us be on time.

Numbers

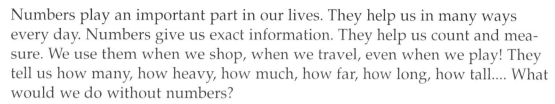

Numbers play an important part in our lives. They help us in many ways every day. Numbers give us exact information. They help us count and measure. We use them when we shop, when we travel, even when we play! They tell us how many, how heavy, how much, how far, how long, how tall.... What would we do without numbers?

Road signs Numbers are very important in giving directions when you travel. Along the roadside there are signs with numbers that identify the highway you are riding on. You can look at a map and match the numbers to find out just where you are. To get where you want to go, you read the numbers of the roads that go there, and choose the best route. Maps also show the number of miles from one town to another. These numbers will give you an idea of how long it will take to get there.

Buying things Numbers give you important information when you want to buy something. On a vending machine, the number over the coin slot tells you how much money to put in. In a store, the numbers on the sign tell you how much the product costs. Then you have the information you need to decide if you want to buy it. You couldn't shop without numbers. Aisle numbers tell you where you are in the supermarket. Numbers on the boxes tell you how many of the item are inside. If you want to buy 20 cookies, look for the number!

Weighing things Scales are for weighing things; the numbers on them tell you how heavy they are. At the grocery store, food is put in the basket of the scale. As the weight pulls the basket down, the pointer on the scale moves to the number that tells you how many pounds and ounces the food weighs. Then you can decide if you want one pound of fruit or maybe two pounds. Scales also weigh people. When you step on the scale, the pointer moves to the number that shows how heavy you are. That number is called your weight.

Playing games Numbers are an important part of most games. The numbers in this hopscotch game tell you where to jump first, then second, and so on. In a game in which one team plays against another, numbers on the uniforms tell you who the players are and numbers keep the score. The team with the higher score wins! Baseball fans record many numbers about their favorite players: how many runs they make each game, how many outs they make, what their batting average is. These baseball numbers are called statistics.

Measuring things You can measure how big something is with a measuring stick that shows feet and inches. The number that tells how tall something is is called its height; how wide is called its width. When you get a checkup at the doctor's office, he will measure your height to see how much you've grown. The number that shows at the top of your head tells him exactly how tall you are. You can use a measuring stick to find out how wide your table is or even the size of a whole room. This information will come in handy if you want to make a tablecloth or get a new bed.

Going places If you need to go someplace, numbers are a big help. Buses are marked with numbers that tell you the route they are going to take. This way, you can choose the right bus to get where you want to go. The sign on the side of the taxi tells you what the fare is: how much it will cost to ride for a certain distance. Other numbers on signs in streets and roads tell you the speed limit, which is how fast your car can go. Numbers also tell you the addresses of different buildings so that you can find the one you're looking for. Numbers will help you find your way if you get lost.

Being on time Clocks help us measure time with hours and minutes. The hands on the clock point to numbers. The big hand tells us the hour and the little hand tells us the minute. When you need to be "on time," reading the numbers on the clock will tell you if you must hurry or if you have plenty of time.